I0471697

The Very Best of

Disguised Limits

Volume #2

by Vincent L. Rogers

Discover Life's Unlimited Opportunities!!!!

Disguised Limits provides you with a wealth of information, resources, and tools that you can use to **Discover Life's Unlimited Opportunities!!!!**

Follow **Disguised Limits** on NetworkedBlogs @ http://networkedblogs.com/blog/disguised_limits and follow me on Twitter @ http://twitter.com/vincevision to receive special updates about networking opportunities, offers and discounts, business and sales leads, plus an abundance of useful tools that you can use to improve every aspect of your life!!!!

www.disguisedlimits.blogspot.com

Vince Rogers Media Ventures
A subsidiary of Vince Rogers & Associates

1st Edition published by **Vince Rogers Media Ventures**

Copyright: © 2012 by **Vincent L. Rogers** *All rights reserved.*
ISBN: 978-1-300-06585-2

No part of this book shall be reproduced, stored, transmitted or copied without written permission from the publisher. This is an original work and is not based on the work of any other writer - living or dead. For more information contact:

Vince Rogers Media Ventures
P.O. Box 77222, Atlanta, GA 30357-1222
United States of America

Challenges are Opportunities... Disguised as Limitations

~ Vincent L. Rogers

Disguised Limits

Discover Life's Unlimited Opportunities!!!!

Persistence

What: **Success**

Who: **You**

How: **Start**

Where: **Here**

When: **Now**

Why: **Persistence**

~ Vincent L. Rogers

Six Keys to Success

1) Information: Become known as a trustworthy subject matter expert in your field.

2) Image: Go out into the world every day and look, speak and act the way you want to be treated.

3) Initiative: Always act on the basis of sound planning and good research, which leads to the pursuit of effective strategy.

4) Confidence: Through dedicating your self to winning small victories, you will be emboldened with the confidence that you've done your best; this will be the basis of the momentum that propels you to success.

5) Capital: The greatest source of future revenue and profits for your business will be determined by the purchasing and cost decisions you make today.

6) Contacts: You must assemble a winning team. You alone will never possess all of the skills and abilities required for perfection, nor will you ever be able to earn every certification or degree needed to answer every question.

Table of Contents

Branding

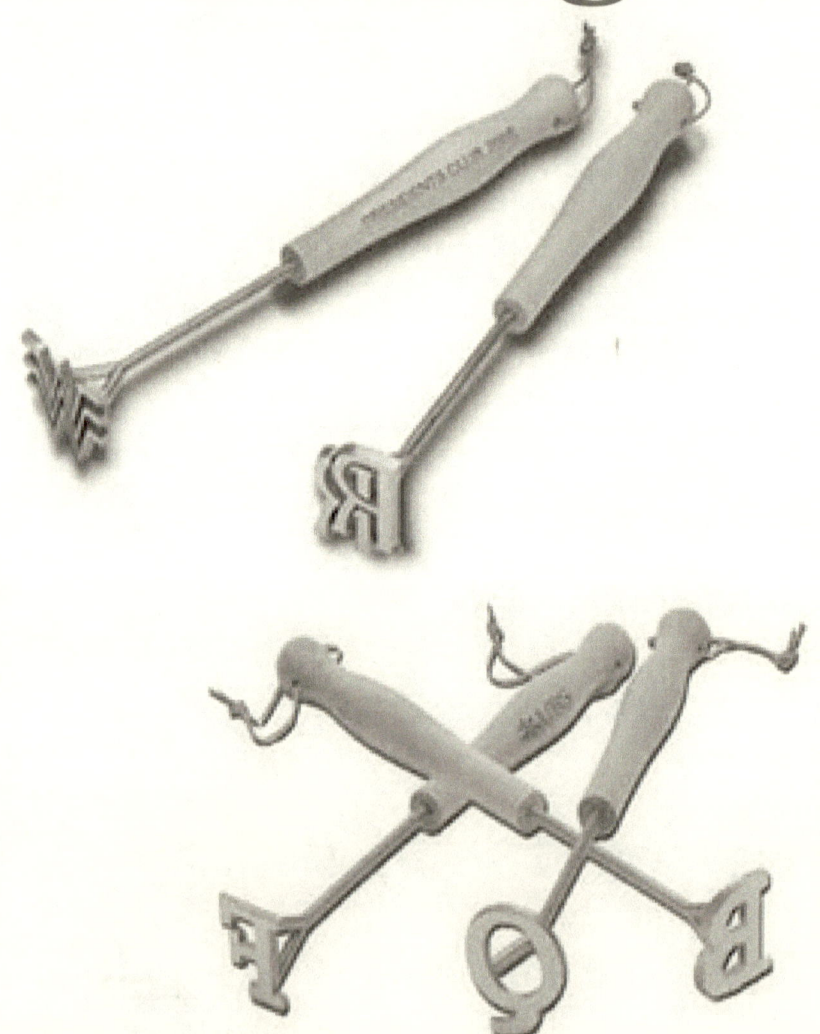

Disguised Limits

Discover Life's Unlimited Opportunities!!!!

From Blog to Book: The Easy Road to "Infopreneurship"

by **Vince Rogers**

It is often said that *content is king* when it comes to building an online presence for your brand. One of the most cost effective and high impact ways to generate and distribute the high quality content that you produce is through publishing a blog. As a subject matter expert in your field, it should not be very difficult to regularly produce high-quality content in order to generate a very informative, well followed blog. The content that you generate and a place to publish it are all that you need to get started on the easy road to "Infopreneurship".

If you are not already blogging, the process for getting started is fairly simple. There are quite a few popular *blog publishing services* that can be used to create your own high quality blog. Some of the more popular outlets are**TypePad**, **Blogger** (which is owned by **Google.com**) and **WordPress**. You can easily determine which of these (or the many other) sites will fit your particular needs. The most common approach to making that decision is through either utilizing trial and error, researching comparisons online or by soliciting referrals from other bloggers.

Personally, I use the Blogger platform to publish my highly popular blog **Disguised Limits** (www.disguisedlimits.blogspot.com) Disguised Limits provides readers with useful articles and special updates about local networking opportunities, offers and discounts, business and sales leads, plus an abundance of other useful business and life enhancing information. When I started to blog, going with the service that had the word blog in the name just made sense to me. You might choose to go with a more scientific approach.

Disguised Limits is the #2 blog in the Opportunities category on**NetwokedBlogs.com**. NetworkedBlogs.com is a blog directory that is maintained by **Facebook.com**. Blog directories are services that list popular blogs, much like an on-line index or card catalog to assist blog followers. Using blog directories enables your blog to gain greater exposure to a wider audience than just relying on being followed by random users of your chosen blog publishing service.

There are also local blogging professionals that can provide you with their expertise to help you build your dynamic blog-based branding machine. Atlanta social media maven **Judi Knight** of **New Tricks** (**www.newtricks.me**) is one of the most sought after and well respected website and blog design experts around town. Knight is a passionate proponent of using social media along with blogging to empower entrepreneurs to *"....capture their "essence" in order to build their brand and grow their businesses...."*

The most well designed and highly informative blog on the internet is nothing without followers. I cannot emphasize strongly enough that the best way to gain a large captive audience of loyal followers is by regularly generating high quality content that is relevant to your target audience. To promote this content and increase their blog's following; most bloggers utilize their existing networks on the most popular social media platforms Twitter, FaceBook, LinkedIn etc. Some other useful tips to growing your blog's readership and fan base are to:

1) Use the blog traffic analytics provided by your blog publishing service to determine the readership patterns of your existing followers.
2) Make widgets or gadgets (apps that link your blog to other websites) available for readers to place on their social media pages, personal websites and personal blogs.
3) Interact with your blog followers by being responsive to their comments on your blog.
4) Follow as many other blogs as you can and regularly interact with other bloggers.

Now that you're the publisher of a successful blog with an avid following, what's next? You are the owner of your blog content and therefore free to publish your articles in any other online and print publications. For most bloggers utilizing their blog to grow their business is more than enough payoff for their effort and ingenuity. However, some savvy bloggers may want to take it a step further by using their blog content to enter the realm of information marketing.

Information marketing is the business of selling Books, e-Books, CDs, DVDs, Webinars Podcasts, etc. to consumers seeking essential knowledge that they can use to enhance their business or professional lives. The most fundamental information products are "inspirational" "motivational" "self-help" or "how-to" books. Turning your blog content into a book provides you with the perfect opportunity to enter the domain of legendary "Infopreneurs" such as Robert Kyosaki, Jim Rohn, Les Brown and Atlanta resident Dennis Kimbro.

The traditional route to getting a book publishing deal is one that you might consider. However, self publishing is the easiest route to bringing your book and or e-book to the public. As with the process of publishing your blog, several easy to use print-on-demand, self publishing sites exist on the internet. Some of the notable names in the game are **Lulu**, **AuthorHouse**, **xLibris** and **iUniverse**. These sites provide users with easy to use tools that allow authors to download simple text documents and images from their own computers to create actual hardcover or paperback books. Within a matter of minutes, you can produce a bookstore quality publication or e-Book that customers can purchase or download from their own computer.

I recently made the great leap into the information marketing space by turning my own blog into a book. **"The Very Best of Disguised Limits"** book is now available to buy or download free at **www.lulu.com** To market and promote your book; you will utilize many of the same tools that are used to market and promote your blog. The book has allowed me to create new business opportunities, expand my number of blog followers and make a few dollars from selling the book as well. The positive response to the book has been more than I ever expected. By following the steps I have outlined, I am sure that in no time flat you can also make the successful conversion from mere mortal blogger to successful Infopreneur "rock star" as well.

"The Very Best of Disguised Limits"

Disguised Limits

Discover Life's Unlimited Opportunities!!!!

Branding Fundamentals: The Golden Rules of Personal Branding

by **Vince Rogers**

Your branding strategy should be viewed as a living, breathing and perpetually evolving entity. Just as with the actions of an actual person, your branding efforts will build a lasting reputation. This reputation is based on people's perception of your brand's appearance, its personality and by how many people have been influenced by your efforts. Your branding strategy irreversibly shapes your public perception, professional reputation and enduring legacy.

Your branding strategy consists of more than just creating a nice logo and printing up some business cards. Although these things are important, they represent only one aspect of your successful branding strategy. Just like an Olympic athlete who strives to stand on the winner's podium, *mastering the fundamentals* is the key to *"Going for the Gold"*. Also like an "Olympian", building a successful branding strategy is governed by adhering to the principles of the *I.O.C.* – **Identity;**

Outreach and Consistency.

There are **3** essential ***Branding Fundamentals*** that make up the

Golden Rules of Personal Branding:

1) Building Your Brand Identity

2) Focusing Your Brand Outreach

3) Maintaining Your Brand Consistency

The Brand Identity Package

Your ***Brand Identity Package*** consists of the tools that you will use to present your brand to the world. The basic components of your brand identity package are a *logo, tagline, business card and letterhead.* In addition to these basic components, most companies will also need a *website or blog and a brochure.* In many instances, the first time that someone receives your business card, letterhead and brochure or views your website and blog; they will make a first and final decision about who you are and what value you bring to the table.

Most people give the creation of their logo primary emphasis when formulating their identity package. Although often neglected, you should give the formulation of your tagline some very serious thought as well. Your tagline serves as a succinct but permanent *Elevator Pitch*. A powerful tagline should communicate your *Unique Selling Proposition (USP)* creatively, but clearly. In other words, it should explain in one sentence what it is that you do and what value you bring to the table.

Reaching Your Target Audience

You've invested a lot of time, money, effort and creativity into creating your brand identity. Now you want people to see what you've done. You really want to impress people with your big title, cool logo and witty tagline. Therefore, you should just give out all of your business cards to every pretty girl you meet at the bar and every old high school friend you run into at the reunion - right? Wrong.

The most effective way to succeed at building your brand is to determine your specific **Target Audience**. The fist step to deciding on your Target Audience is to create a profile of your **Ideal Customer**. Once you have done this, you should try as much as possible to reach those people and only those people with your message. This will be the key to success of your well focused brand outreach strategy.

Always Be Consistently Consistent

It has been said that the only thing constant in life is change. On the other hand, it is also fairly clear that most people don't really like change. It is an absolute fact that the worst thing you can do when trying to build your brand is to keep changing the message. You should use the same images and value propositions consistently across all marketing channels.

Channels overlap frequently in today's complex marketing environment. The tagline on your business card can't communicate that you're the "low cost leader", but the tagline on your website says something different. Whether it's colors, graphics or taglines; constantly changing the elements of you brand identity leads to confusion. Confusion leads to uncertainty -

uncertainty leads to risk. Ultimately, this perception of risk will lead to your prospects choosing the competition.

Some factors that you should consider in order to insure your brand consistency are to:

1) Use the Same Graphics Elements Across All Mediums

2) Formulate a Core Message and Stick With It

3) Always Communicate Your *Unique Selling Proposition*

4) Separate Business from Personal When Using Social Media

You should adapt your message to changing conditions if the essential elements of your branding strategy actually change. However, you should avoid making changes in order to chase trends or just to suit a single prospective client. Instead, when "going for the gold" you should always remember to adhere to the rules of the ***I.O.C.*** and stick to the fundamentals by playing by the "golden rules". Build a unique brand **Identity,** focus your brand's **Outreach** and maintain your brand's **Consistency.**

Disguised Limits

Discover Life's Unlimited Opportunities!!!!

Building Your "Standout" Brand as a Consultant

by **Vince Rogers**

"I am a consultant." This declaration is probably heard more these days than the answer to the question "What is your name?" More than at any other time in history, this economy has prompted well educated highly skilled professionals to seek to earn a living by plying their trade without working for an employer. So how does the "standout" consultant rise above the masses of tenderfoot claimants who are just temporarily between jobs? Conversely, how can bright new consultants convince prospective clients that they are really tuned-in and not just singing the same old song?

The consulting trend is especially evident in a city like Atlanta. According to the Georgia Department of Labor, as of October 2011, the Metro Atlanta unemployment rate stood at 10.3%. That is more than a point above the national average. Yet many of these unemployed people are well trained and highly qualified. More importantly, the need for their skills has not disappeared. Most of these people were simply "laid off" in order for the company to cut the costs of salaries and benefits. Now these companies are challenged to continue to increase productivity with less manpower and faced with diminished brainpower.

Many of these displaced workers were key management and executive level employees. Because of their high salaries and the fact that there are fewer openings for top-level positions, they may have limited success finding a new job at the same level. In order to earn a living, out of necessity these former long-time employees are faced with the daunting task of becoming first time entrepreneurs.

Given the economic trends concerning workforce expansion and economic productivity, hiring consultants as opposed to full-time employees is becoming the rule rather than the exception. Translation: This isn't your grandmother's workforce. Progressively more opportunities to become a consultant may become available in the future than permanent full-time jobs created. According to Atlanta technology and publishing consultant **Leo Tucker**, author of the book *__Free Agent Executive__* *"Contractors or consultants are at the forefront of a revolution in the workforce."*

So what does it take to gain a foothold as a consultant in this current environment? Essentially all consultants have to do 3 things to succeed:

1) Define your area of expertise
2) Find Clients
3) Deliver a quality product
   Numbers 1 and 3 will be determined by the experiences and abilities that you have acquired throughout your career. Number 2 will be a function of your efforts to effectively build and promote your brand in order to stand out from the competition.

When you walk into your local Home Depot in search of a new hammer, you assume the hammer is a good one because of the quality you expect from the Home Depot brand. To gain this same level of confidence from your prospective clients will require you to create the perception that your generic skills are of a higher quality than the identical skills presented by the next guy. This seems like it could be a daunting task. However, by employing a few strategies you can manage to stand out from the crowd.

As a reminder, there are 3 *Branding Fundamentals* that should always guide your *Branding Strategy*:

1) Build your Brand **Identity**

2) Maintain your Brand **Consistency**

3) Focus your Branding **Outreach**

The image you present through your marketing materials (business cards, correspondence, website, etc.) is very important. The information this *"identity package"* transfers to the public are the first signs of your dedication to quality. What these materials communicate will be the first signs that the potential client receives as to the soundness of your thinking. Making sure these simple things create a lasting impression will help potential clients remember you instead of the other guy.

In this day and age you must build and manage a quality online reputation. There are a number of well known platforms available for establishing an online presence. However, most business people drop the ball when it comes to monitoring and managing their internet presence. The analytic tools of your various pages and blogs should be evaluated regularly to make sure you are consistently reaching your target market. Using online tools and social media better than the next guy will definitely give you a leg up on the competition.

Another vital yet overlooked key to successful branding is building and managing the right relationships. Who you associate with and are associated with can make more of a lasting impression than you ever could by attempting to make your own unassisted introduction to a prospect. A referral from someone your client already knows and respects can be the key to opening the door to new business. Sometimes, it really does come down to who you know.

In summary, to attract customers as a consultant in this competitive environment you will have to stand out from the competition. Once you determine your area of specialization and determine the niche market that you will service, finding clients will be your greatest challenge. To be successful at building your business, you will have to build a brand that stands out from the competition. The keys to successfully leveraging that brand will be determined by maintaining the consistently of the brand and continuously engaging your target market.

Vince Rogers is the **Principal Change Agent** at **Vince Rogers & Associates**
www.vincerogers.biz

He has been profiled in such business media outlets as High Velocity Radio
http://highvelocityradio.businessradiox.com/2010/12/vince-rogers-enterpise-optimization
and Write Here, Write Now
http://writeherewritenow.businessradiox.com/?powerpress_pinw=198-podcast

His book **"The Very Best of Disguised Limits"**

is available to buy or download free @ **http://www.lulu.com/product/paperback/the-very-best-of-disguised-limits/16215088**
and is also available @ **Amazon.com**

Disguised Limits

Discover Life's Unlimited Opportunities!!!!

"Re-Branding" Yourself When Facing Adversity

You graduate from a historic and prestigious university. You land your dream job in the glamorous entertainment industry. You work directly with a music legend and famous celebrities. You are regarded in your profession as a highly talented and extremely energetic "*go-getter*". You become a Vice-President at one of the most iconic brand names in the entertainment industry. You are regarded as a real "*Big Deal*". You have it all.

You are diagnosed with Multiple Sclerosis (*MS*) at the age of 22. For years you manage to hide the debilitating limitations the condition imposes on you. Nevertheless, you devote 15 years to building an identity that is synonymous with confidence, competence and consistency. You accomplish all of this under the most challenging circumstances. But ultimately, the pressures of the fast paced, stressful world of the entertainment industry become too much to manage. This eventually leads to you being laid off from a job that has been your identity for more than a decade. You've lost it all. Now what?

*Six years ago, Atlanta based **Personal Brand Strategy** coach **Kelly Green** was faced with this exact dilemma. The simultaneous challenges of managing her serious health condition and the loss of her high-status career seriously shook the core of her identity. She affirms that*

"When I got laid off, I was hurt, angry and embarrassed, but most of all I had no idea what I was going to do next!"

After no small amount of soul searching, she decided for the first time in her life to put a priority on her own personal well being. This was not easy for someone who was used to putting their career first. As she puts it, "*My ego wanted to continue living the lifestyle I had been living for 15 years, but deep down I knew that I needed a mental and physical break from it all.*"

This realization highlights the first stage of what "**Coach Kelly**" characterizes as the process of "**Personal Re-Branding**" Many people are currently facing the process of repositioning their lives after facing serious adversities. Home foreclosure, job loss, severe illness and other major challenges can send a persons life into a tailspin. Not only can such life altering adversities affect how the world sees your personal brand identity, but they can deeply alter your personal self-image as well. Kelly believes that the first question you have to ask yourself in this process of personal "re-branding" is

"What do I want to do with my life now and how does my new situation affect that?"

She realized that if she was going to continue pursuing her dreams, she would first have to address her health situation. During this process she met with a Holistic Nutrition Coach while still residing in New York City. Not only was this encounter beneficial to her health, it also helped her identify the path she should take towards "*re-branding*" herself professionally. Luckily for us, she also decided to relocate to Atlanta to pursue what she describes as a "*better quality of life*".

Based on her experiences with wellness professionals, Kelly went on to become a **Certified Wellness Coach** herself. However in an "*Aha Moment*" she ascertained that her client's needs went beyond their emotional and physical wellness. She realized that they also needed help "*developing and clarifying their Brand*". Her years of experience in Marketing and her passion for helping people motivated her to combine these abilities to also become a **Personal Branding Strategist**.

The marketing of entertainers had been her job function in the fast-paced music industry. However, she realized that essentially her true passion was helping people realize their full potential. As she states it, she identified that there were other "*People just like me who needed to "re-brand" and needed to build a new identity.*"

Identifying your true passion and unique skills are essential to the "*re-branding*" process. This is true whether you find yourself facing the best of life's good fortune or the hardest of life's bad times. Some other key steps to follow in this process that Green has identified are:

- Position yourself as an expert regarding what you are passionate about.
- Identify a targeted niche population that needs your unique skills.
- Create a profile of an ideal client that needs your services. (Be Specific)
- Understand your **Unique Selling Proposition (USP)** that appeals to your ideal client.

Kelly emphasizes that understanding your *Unique Selling Proposition (USP)* is the key to understanding how to convert your passion into an actual income generating enterprise. Having faced great adversity herself enabled Green to embrace one of the most essential components to developing your *USP*. You must be able to

"....Speak to a potential client's "Pain Point" and demonstrate that you are uniquely qualified to solve their problem...."

An organization's "***Pain Point***" is defined as an area in which they are having trouble fulfilling a consumer's need. Green believes that her ability to empathize with people who are searching to establish or re-establish their identity is one of the keys to her success. "*I've seen what it's like when you don't understand your brand and how things open up when you do*" she says.

This process of "*re-branding*" has value not just for Green's customers who are mostly entrepreneurs and "*solo-service*" professionals. Developing your Personal Brand and identifying your *USP* can be useful for job seekers, career changers and even for people making a decision about academic pursuits. This is especially true when facing adversity.

Green firmly believes that you "*Don't be afraid to take the first steps no matter what the outcome will be.*" This process can be a totally individual effort, or it may require that you seek the guidance of a mentor or **Branding Coach**. In any event, Kelly believes that

"In order to communicate your value to other people, you have to know and understand your value first."

To learn more about Kelly Green please visit www.insiderbrandingsecrets.com or contact her at kelly@insiderbrandingsecrets.com

Continue reading on Examiner.com "Re-Branding" Yourself When Facing Adversity - Atlanta personal brand | Examiner.com http://www.examiner.com/personal-brand-in-atlanta/re-branding-yourself-when-facing-adversity#ixzz1sLEBVvWT

Disguised Limits

Discover Life's Unlimited Opportunities!!!!

A Personal Branding Strategy for Your Career Search
By **Vince Rogers**

In this turbulent economy, companies still face the challenge of maximizing productivity. Essential to achieving that mission is making cost effective, purchase decisions that add value to the "bottom line". Effective managers must maximize return on investment from every resource – especially human resources. Therefore, making excellent hiring decisions is critical to achieving the success of an organization.

The goal of employers in today's job market is to find the "ideal" candidate for every job opening. Facing a "lean" job market, the goal of every jobseeker should be to present themselves as the ideal candidate for a specific career opportunity. From the employer's perspective, finding the right person for a job is not just a hiring decision – it is also a purchase decision. Therefore, it is imperative that you package yourself in a way that makes you more attractive than all of the other "products" available in the marketplace.

Employers want to know more than whether you can simply do the job. It is also necessary that you can align with the mission, values and philosophy of the company. Are you an *Experienced I.T. Professional* or a *Technology Industry Change Agent*? Different organizations may require or desire one or the other. However if you're not the right fit for the specific opportunity you're applying for, the savvy hiring manager will know. Most importantly, you don't want to waste your time applying for one position, if you are really better suited to another one that is available elsewhere. Many unfocused jobseekers apply over and over again for positions that they're not suited for, expecting to sneak in the back door. Well here's an important newsflash – savvy employers aren't "buying it".

It is essential that you identify and effectively communicate your *Brand Promise*. This is your statement or statements that combine what you are, with what you can deliver to the company. Anybody can say *"I am a hard working professional who has produced quality results"* and many people make such generic statements all of the time. My advice is that you go in another direction. I would suggest something more like: *"I am a Technology Industry Change Agent who works well with teams and independently, to solve complex problems and maximize the productivity of a dynamic I.T. Department."* This type of Brand Promise distinguishes your uniqueness and establishes the value you will bring to the organization.

In addition to creating a customized resume and cover letter for each position, you should also be prepared to make a full presentation of your entire *Career Portfolio*. Written letters of recommendation; copies of awards and certificates as well as documentation of academic achievements should be made available upon the request of the prospective employer. All of these items can be compiled into a *"Brag Book"* A "Brag Book" is a binder or folder containing documentation of your academic and career accomplishments that you can present to a job interviewer. It effectively serves the same presentation function as a businesses portfolio, which one company would provide to another in a Business to Business or *"B2B"* setting.

In the final analysis, an individual must undertake many of the same steps to get their next job as a business does in order to get their next client. So just like a businessperson, you should also create a business card and start actively networking. Although "Job Boards", social and professional networking sites and even blogging are great outlets for showcasing your personal brand, most new career opportunities are discovered through "face-to-face" Networking. Nevertheless, whether it is online or in person, utilizing the aforementioned strategies will set you apart from the competition in the execution of an effective personal branding strategy for career success.

Get the Latest News and Information on Personal Branding in Atlanta from

Vince Rogers - Atlanta's Personal Branding Expert!!!!

www.examiner.com/x-60388-Atlanta-Personal-Brand-Examiner

Disguised Limits

Discover Life's Unlimited Opportunities!!!!

Connecting Mission to Brand: The Evolution of a Modern Non-Profit

"Growing small and medium-sized minority owned businesses is one of the best ways to close the wealth gap in America."

Marc H. Morial, President and CEO, National Urban League

In 1920, the *National Urban League* assumed its current formal name. This national organization was created through the consolidation of several prominent empowerment organizations of that era. They adopted as their mission, *"to enable African Americans to secure economic self-reliance, parity, power and civil rights."* The Atlanta chapter – the *Atlanta Urban League* was also formed that same year.

Most people usually associate an effective branding strategy with *creating identity (brand awareness)* and *establishing image*. In the case of a non-profit organization, effective branding must accomplish much more than that. The branding strategy must also be carefully aligned with the mission and values of the organization. A successful branding strategy must also facilitate the expansion of the organization's *operating capacity (capacity building)* and be representative of the organization's *social impact*.

Successful modern non-profits must evolve. When they do, they must also make sure that their branding strategy be connected to their renewed mission. The mission of the Urban League has always been economic empowerment and civil rights. The primary measurement of the organization's social impact was finding job opportunities for their constituency. The Urban League realized that simply securing job opportunities in this evolving economy did not effectively address their mission. The "League" has responded to changing times and identified that the true measurement of success should now be establishing businesses and creating jobs. At the vanguard of realizing this renewed mission is the *Atlanta Entrepreneurship Center* **www.aultec.org**

Providing dynamic leadership at the helm of the Atlanta Entrepreneurship Center is their *Executive Director – Mr. Marc Parham.* As he so eloquently and succinctly states, *"Finding people jobs has always been the mission of the Urban League"*, but this was essentially a process of negotiating for or demanding jobs from mainstream employers. This was necessary to redress inequities that developed because of past civil rights and social welfare injustices. However, according to Parham the charge of the organization as a modern non-profit is to now *"Create jobs via entrepreneurship"*.

The Atlanta Entrepreneurship Center is one very important component of a holistic approach to providing economic empowerment programs to the National Urban Leagues' constituency. The Entrepreneurship

Center (TEC) was launched in Atlanta in October 2004. At the core of the program is education via four primary methods. These essential training programs are as follows:

- Start-up Business Essentials Series for Entrepreneurs
- Existing Business Series – Writing The Business Plan
- Specialized Workshops - Focusing on specific topics (i.e. QuickBooks, Websites, Insurance, Access to Capital, etc)
- Group or One on One Coaching – Experienced Business Consultants will meet one on one with participants to coach them with the development of their business plan.

The different components are designed to suit the needs of start-up, early stage and long-established business. The *Start-up Business Essentials Series* is a six (6) session series that helps entrepreneurs to understand the basic business essentials for starting a business. The *Existing Business Series* curriculum is devoted to giving entrepreneurs a foundation in the *"Core 4 Systems"* which are:

- Success Planning
- Marketing Planning
- Cash-flow Planning
- Operations Planning

While for-profit *"business incubators"* may offer similar services, a non-profit is uniquely positioned to provide participants with additional value added components. They can offer a high caliber of business acumen, lower cost and provide other "supportive services'. Many top-notch Atlanta business consultants make themselves available to students as their way of "giving back". According to Parham, *"People who work at the Urban League, really understand, the plight of the people that they work with because they've walked in their shoes."* Essentially this means that they have also experienced all of the ups and downs of building a successful business. They are motivated to share their wealth of knowledge in order to help other people succeed, not by the prospect of personal gain.

In developing a branding strategy for a non-profit, it may be necessary to first undertake a *SWOT Analysis* of the organization. SWOT stands for *Strengths, Weaknesses, Opportunities and Threats.* This is important in order to access whether reengineering the branding strategy could possibly undermine the already established *brand equity* of the organization. Brand equity is the value that a company realizes in the public from positive associations by consumers compared to their competition. In the case of a non-profit organization, alienating long time supporters could possibly alienate existing supporters and damage the ability to realize ongoing *social impact*. Providing social impact is ultimately the purpose of an effective non-profit.

In the case of a non-profit, not all of the impacts are always tangibly measureable. Mr. Parham asserts that a significant aspect of aligning the branding strategy of the Atlanta Entrepreneurship Center to their mission is to *"Give people the confidence that they can succeed."* Unlike a business, accomplishing an intangible goal such as this enhances brand equity and is an important sign that a non-profit organization is succeeding. Enhancing brand equity while demonstrating social impact is ultimately the goal of connecting mission to brand.

Disguised Limits

Discover Life's Unlimited Opportunities!!!!

Place Branding - The Case for "Yo Boulevard!"

by **Vince Rogers**

Place Branding is a fairly new concept in the branding *"discipline"*. The term refers to the process of communicating a well-crafted image to a target audience in order to create a specific perception of a particular place. Most often place branding is the aide-decamp of Branding's close relative – Reputation Management. Reputation Management is the process of formulating a positive image or repairing a negative image of a brand. Most often a brand accrues a bad reputation following a negative event or unfortunate change in circumstances.

In the case of a place, whether it is a nation, a city or a neighborhood, this bad reputation usually evolves over time. It ultimately can lead to losses of population, declining economic activity and high crime rates. A negative perception can be associated with a place for years, even if the facts don't support the perception. This in summary is what has become the plight of Atlanta's Old Fourth Ward.

The neighborhood is home to Martin Luther King, Jr.'s childhood home, Ebenezer Baptist Church and in years past, was considered a very desirable residential location in Atlanta. Today the principal through street in this community - Boulevard, has earned a reputation for facilitating every urban vice imaginable. According to Kwanza Hall the presiding Atlanta City Councilmember for the district, it is *"the most concentrated pocket of poverty in the southeastern United States."*

There are several cities in America such as Detroit on the negative end of the spectrum and Miami on the positive end of the spectrum that have experienced a change in perception over the years. So what can be done to change the perception of a place when the fortunes of the community have reversed? There are essentially 4 Key Steps to a implementing a successful Place Branding Strategy:

1.   **Assemble a Diverse Team of Advisers**
2.   **Partner with the Business Community in the surrounding area**
3.   **Concentrate on Achieving Key Objectives**
4.   **Leverage Existing Community Assets**

TEDx Atlanta - The Birth of the Yo Boulevard! Brand

In March of 2012, Councilman Hall was as an attendee at a TEDx
Atlanta www.tedxatlanta.com conference. Surrounded by some of the best and brightest minds in the city, it dawned on him that he should seize the opportunity to seek confederates for his campaign to restore civility to Boulevard. In January, Hall had already declared 2012 the *"Year of Boulevard"*. It was at the conference that the brand name *"Yo Boulevard!"* www.yoboulevard.com evolved and became a living breathing entity. The association with TEDx Atlanta served the purpose of gaining access to a diverse source of advisers with vast intellectual capital. It also provided the potential for partnerships with the city's most progressive business leaders who possessed the necessary physical and financial capital.

The Children Are Our Future

Hall determined that the most important objective that should be pursued was empowering the children who lived in the community to break the *"cycle of poverty"*. He decided to focus on the children as the key objective because he believes that *"You can change all the physical structures, but if you haven't given people real opportunities, all you're going to do is push them out."* Borne out of the TEDx conference, a three (3) part challenge was issued to the business and community leaders in the community:

1. **Sponsor a child for summer camp**
2. **Hire a child for a summer internship**
3. **Help a young person start a business and become an entrepreneur**

During what was termed as the *"Summer of Possibility"* in association with their diverse team of advisers and by leveraging local businesses and vital community assets, Yo Boulevard! achieved all three objectives.

Operation PEACE: A Diamond in a Rough Place

Facing the onslaught of "gentrification" and the specter of past "urban renewal" schemes, it is unlikely that the residents in the Boulevard corridor would have welcomed warmly a new round of infiltration by people they consider "outsiders". Even the inroads of more affluent or well educated residents of the adjacent communities might be met with skepticism without the intercession of an established and trusted force in the community. The natural candidate to fill this role in the Boulevard community was Operation P.E.A.C.E. www.operationpeace.org

Under the steadfast and trusted leadership of Executive Director, Ms. Edna Moffett, since 1995 Operation P.E.A.C.E. has been a dynamic agent of change in an otherwise neglected community. Operation P.E.A.C.E began as an effort to improve the lives of the children in the Old Fourth Ward community. In addition to serving as a buffer between the neighborhood children and the negative forces at work in the community, the organization has evolved into the primary community resource for residents looking for solutions to their problems. According to Moffet, *"Because of our long track record as a catalyst for change in the community and a driver of successful outcomes for our youth, it was decided that Operation P.E.A.C.E. should be the standard-bearer for Yo Boulevard!"*

"Living Laboratory for Innovation"

Only time, effort and "right action" will determine whether Yo Boulevard! can effectively counteract years of negative perceptions of the Old Fourth Ward community and the infamous Boulevard corridor. Hall's stated goal is to convert the community into a *"Living Laboratory for Innovation". His* prudent insight and stalwart commitment to the project are evidenced by his observations that *"We're talking about changing something that's been in place for thirty years. It's not going to change in six months."* Although place branding initiatives have an inherent idealistic quality, with the type of pragmatic leadership that Councilman Hall provides to the project, it stands an excellent chance of succeeding.

Yo Boulevard! | SUMMER OF POSSIBILITY |

Any successful branding strategy requires the dedication of adequate time, resources and organization. In the case of Place Branding, it is best to move moderately rather than be overly aggressive. The alliances that have been forged can be broken and confidences of the various stakeholders can be easily eroded. Yet if managed properly, an area that was thought to have already seen its best days can be transformed into a vigorous, lively and productive community.

Disguised Limits

Discover Life's Unlimited Opportunities!!!!

Using Expert Videos to Build Your Brand

by **Vince Rogers**

YOU'VE REACHED THE PINNACLE OF YOUR PROFESSION. NOW YOU WANT TO CONTINUE BUILDING YOUR BRAND BY SHARING YOUR EXPERTISE ON THE "BIG SCREEN". OKAY MAYBE WE'LL START WITH COMPUTER MONITORS AND "SMARTPHONES" AND WORK OUR WAY UP TO THE BIG SCREEN LATER. LIGHTS; CAMERAS; ACTION! – YOU'RE READY TO MAKE A PROFESSIONALLY PRODUCED EXPERT VIDEO.

I WAS RECENTLY CALLED UPON TO DO JUST THAT, BY FILMING A "BUSINESS SUCCESS" VIDEO SERIES FOR EHOW.COM. ALTHOUGH THE EXPERIENCE WAS PERSONALLY AND PROFESSIONALLY REWARDING, IT WAS CERTAINLY NO "WALK IN THE PARK". MANY ELEMENTS GO INTO MAKING A HIGH QUALITY VIDEO THAT PRESENTS YOUR BRAND IN THE BEST LIGHT. YOU MUST SELECT THE RIGHT TOPIC FOR YOUR AUDIENCE, REFINE YOUR CONTENT FOR EFFECTIVE PRESENTATION AND ALSO CHOOSE THE RIGHT LOCATION IN ORDER TO PRODUCE A HIGH QUALITY FINISHED PRODUCT. MOST IMPORTANTLY, YOU MUST WORK WITH A HIGHLY EXPERIENCED, TECHNICALLY PROFICIENT, AND CREATIVELY PERCEPTIVE FILMMAKER.

THE FILMMAKER FOR MY PROJECT CERTAINLY FIT THE BILL. ATLANTA FILMMAKER EDWARD CASTNER HAS 20+ YEARS OF EXPERIENCE IN ALL ASPECTS OF FILM PRODUCTION CAMERA WORK AND FILM EDITING. SOME OF HIS PREVIOUS PROJECTS INCLUDE WORK FOR THE DISCOVERY CHANNEL, NATIONAL GEOGRAPHIC CHANNEL, BBC, ITN AND THE NATIONAL GALLERY OF ART. HE ALSO SPENT THREE WEEKS IN NEW ORLEANS COVERING THE AFTERMATH OF HURRICANE KATRINA. EVEN BEFORE THE ACTUAL VIDEO SHOOT TOOK PLACE, ED WAS INSTRUMENTAL IN ADVISING ME TO CREATE VISUAL AIDS THAT WOULD ENHANCE MY ORAL PRESENTATION. ACCORDING TO ED, "MOST PEOPLE FAIL TO REALIZE HOW IMPORTANT STRONG VISUALS ARE TO THE EFFECTIVENESS OF A GOOD VIDEO."

THE ACTUAL "FILMIC" ELEMENTS OF THE VIDEO ARE NOT THE ONLY DETAILS YOU MUST PAY ATTENTION TO. WHEN MAKING AN "EXPERT" VIDEO, YOUR APPEARANCE AND PRESENTATION ARE STILL THE MOST ESSENTIAL ELEMENTS. YOU SHOULD PAY CLOSE ATTENTION TO THE FOLLOWING PERSONAL DETAILS:

1) WEAR ATTIRE THAT IS WELL SUITED TO YOUR LEVEL OF EXPERTISE

2) MAKE SURE THAT YOUR VOICE AND LANGUAGE ARE TAILORED TO YOUR AUDIENCE

3) LIMIT THE LENGTH OF YOUR VIDEO TO THE MINIMUM TIME NEEDED TO EXPLAIN THE TOPIC

4) TRY TO BE AWARE OF YOUR FACIAL EXPRESSIONS, POSTURE AND BODY LANGUAGE

EVEN WITH ED'S PATIENCE AND PROFESSIONALISM, I STILL FOUND THE EXPERIENCE OF MAKING MY FIRST VIDEOS MUCH HARDER THAN I ANTICIPATED. GETTING USED TO THE CAMERA AS YOUR ONLY AUDIENCE IS A CHALLENGE TO SAY THE LEAST. GETTING USED TO THE PENETRATING HOT LIGHTS BURNING RIGHT THROUGH YOU IS ANOTHER MATTER ALTOGETHER. IT WOULD HAVE BEEN ALMOST IMPOSSIBLE TO MANAGE THIS PROCESS WITHOUT THE HELP OF A SEASONED PROFESSIONAL FILMMAKER.

IF YOU WOULD LIKE TO CONTACT ED CASTNER TO CAPTURE YOUR BRAND AND EXPERTISE ON FILM YOU MAY CONTACT HIM AT WWW.EDCASTNER.COM/CONTACT

TO VIEW THE FINISHED PRODUCT OF OUR VIDEO SHOOT VISIT HTTP://WWW.EHOW.COM/VIDEOS-ON_12239455_BUSINESS-SUCCESS.HTML

Business Success

Disguised Limits

Discover Life's Unlimited Opportunities!!!!

Business Success Video Series
Presented by **Vince Rogers** for

Today's business marketplace is as competitive as ever, so it's always important to use whatever you can to get ahead and stand out from the competition.

Learn about the

Keys to business Success

with help from the

Principal Change Agent at

Vince Rogers & Associates

in this free video series.

www.ehow.com/videos-on_12239455_business-success.html

Disguised Limits

Discover Life's Unlimited Opportunities!!!!

What Has Marketing Provided to Our Economy and Our Lives?

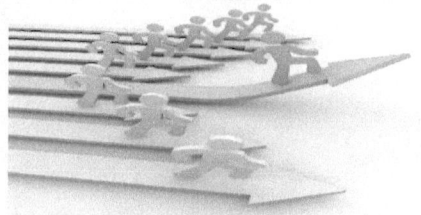

by Vince Rogers

Marketing is defined by the American Marketing Association as *"the activities, institutions, and processes that create, communicate, deliver, and exchange products and services that provide value to businesses, consumers, and society at large."* The benefits that Marketing activities such as Advertising, Public Relations and Sales Promotion provides to businesses are pretty easy to understand. These activities help companies to; Increase Revenue; Maximize Sales; and Attract Customers. So what's in it for us?

Marketing helps to create Competition between companies. Competition between companies results in *3 Major Benefits to Consumers*. These benefits are **1)** Promotion of Good Customer Service; **2)** Availability of a Wide Variety of Products and Services and **3)** Lower Prices for Consumers.

Companies use marketing activities to *Promote Good Customer* Service. They must make good on their claims of providing good customer service in order to satisfy their customers. Companies know that if they promote good customer service, but don't make good on that promise, they will lose their customers to the competition.

Competition between firms results in the availability of an almost unlimited *Wide Variety of Products and Services* being produced and made available to consumers. Companies are constantly creating and promoting new varieties of products to compete for market share with their competition. This abundance enables consumers to have access to options that best suit their specific needs and tastes.

Maybe most important to consumers is the fact that competitive marketing activities between companies results in *Lower Prices for Consumers*. Because competing products usually have similar prices, marketing is used to promote discounts, coupons, rebates or any other price incentives. These attributes are designed to lure customers away from competing products. Also, companies use marketing to promote other non-price differences between competitor's products and services such as new features, free shipping, extended warranties or anything else that will appeal to targeted consumers.

The benefits that marketing provides to businesses and consumers helps to expand the economy by making sure that consumers are provided with a wide variety of well priced products and good customer service. These factors help to create a strong economy that produces successful businesses, low unemployment, and sufficient tax revenue to provide people with essential government services. All of these factors combined should contribute a higher quality of life for all of us.

This article is a companion to the **"Business Success" Video Series** presented
by **Vince Rogers** for eHow.com
http://www.ehow.com/videos-on_12239455_business-success.html

Learn about the **Keys to Business Success** with help from the

VINCE ROGERS
Resources Management
& Communications Consultants
& ASSOCIATES

Principal Change Agent at

Vince Rogers & Associates www.vincerogers.biz

Disguised Limits

Discover Life's Unlimited Opportunities!!!!

What Are Two Common Barriers That Prevent Firms From Entering a Market?
by Vince Rogers

Many people dream of starting a new business. Many of us will succeed in getting that new business off the ground. Unfortunately, many of these businesses will fail. For those businesses that never get off the ground; there are a number of *"Barriers to Entry"* that prevent these enterprises from launching.

There are many barriers to entry into a market that new companies can face such as:

- Lack of Access to Proprietary Technology

- Government Regulations or Bureaucratic "Red Tape"

- Zoning Issues

- Existing Customer Loyalty for Competing Products

However there are Two Common Barriers That Prevent Most Firms from Entering a Market. This is true whether you're trying to open a typical fast food franchise or an innovative high tech start-up. They are *Lack of Access to Sufficient Startup Capital* and *Lack of a Solid Business Plan*.

It is often said that the number one reason for business failure is lack of access to sufficient operating capital. *Lack of Access to Sufficient Startup Capital* is the number one reason that most businesses never get off the ground. If you don't have personal savings to fund your Business, then you will have to acquire it from other sources. The most common sources of business financing are:

- Family

- Friends

- Banks

- Venture Capital Firms & "Angel Investors"

Financing from most of these sources will come in the form of loans that will have to be repaid. *Venture Capitalists or "Angel Investors"* will seek to acquire some percentage of ownership interest and control. However, sometimes aspiring entrepreneurs simply can't obtain the necessary funding to start their business. In many of those cases, the one thing that they often fail to accept is that their concept or idea just may not be ready to be a real business.

If you can't acquire the funding to launch your new business you might want to consider the obvious – your concept may not be strong enough to be an actual business yet. The second most prominent barrier to market entry is Lack of a Solid Business Plan. Having a great concept without a solid business plan can be a significant barrier to business success. A well written business plan helps to guide you through each step of the process in formulating your business. If you are seeking to get funding from sources such as Banks, the SBA, Venture Capital firms or even your relatives, you're going to need a high quality written business plan

If you don't have enough money to fund your business from the concept stage through initial operations it is highly unlikely that your business will be able to get of the ground. If you don't have a solid business plan you won't have the roadmap you need for business success. Also, without a well written business plan it is unlikely that you will be able to acquire the additional capital you may need to succeed.

VINCE ROGERS
Resources Management
& Communications Consultants

& ASSOCIATES

This article is a companion to the "Business Success" Video Series presented by Vince Rogers for eHow.com http://www.ehow.com/videos-on_12239455_business-success.html

Learn about the Keys to business Success with help from the Principal Change Agent at Vince Rogers & Associates www.vincerogers.biz

Disguised Limits

Discover Life's Unlimited Opportunities!!!!

What Do Marketers Need to Know to Reach their Target Audience?

by **Vince Rogers**

There are essentially *2* different types of *Marketing Strategy Approaches*. There is *Mass Marketing* which involves delivering your message via a broadcast marketing channel such as television. You do this in hope that the message will reach consumers in all of the different *Market Segments* for your product or service. Then there is *Target Marketing* which involves *aiming* your marketing efforts towards reaching a well-defined *Target Audience*

The *Target Audience* is a segment of the *Target Market* that has common characteristics. The most effective way to succeed at marketing a specific product or service is to determine your specific Target Audience for that product or service. If you are marketing boxing gloves for instance, your target market is boxers. Deciding on the best target audience may require some research.

The fist step to deciding on a *Target Audience* is to create a profile of your *Target Customer*. This profile should provide for a description of your *Ideal Customer*. Some of the characteristics to determine in building your ideal customer profile are: *Geographic Considerations*: Where do they live? *Demographic Considerations*: What Are their Age, Sex, Occupation etc. *and Psychographic Consideration*: What do they believe in?

If you're selling boxing gloves the most important question to ask may be whether individual boxers or some other Target Audience is going to be the best to focus your marketing efforts on? For instance, the end user for our boxing gloves is obviously the boxer. However, the Coach, Trainer, Gym Owner or Athletic Association may be the actual buyer or decision maker. As a Marketer you should focus your resources towards reaching the Target Audience that you believe is likely to buy the most boxing gloves.

Determining the Target Audience for your Marketing Campaign will help you determine the most cost effective way to deliver the right marketing message. To deliver that message you must use the appropriate marketing channel. These are the keys to success of implementing your successful Target Marketing Strategy.

This article is a companion to the **"Business Success"** **Video Series** presented by **Vince Rogers** for eHow.com **http://www.ehow.com/videos-on_12239455_business-success.html**

Learn about the **Keys to business Success** with help from the **Principal Change Agent** at

VINCE ROGERS
Resources Management
& Communications Consultants
& ASSOCIATES   Vince Rogers & Associates **www.vincerogers.biz**

Disguised Limits

Discover Life's Unlimited Opportunities!!!!

How to Make a Customer Feel Welcomed

by **Vince Rogers**

Businesses that focus on providing a *Positive Customer Experience* are the most likely to experience *Long-Term Success.* Companies that do a good job of *Satisfying Customers* focus on the *Customer's Needs.* The goals of your marketing efforts should be to *Create Initial Awareness* with potential customers. After they are *Converted into Actual Customers* the company should then seek to *Cultivate a Long Term Relationship.*

The Brand Ambassador

The goal of gaining a *Satisfied Customer* should be to convert them into a *Life-Long Loyal Customer.* The first step to creating a satisfied customer is *Providing a Quality Product or Service.* Your product or service must Deliver *the Value* that the customer expects.

How do you know whether the customer is satisfied with your product or service? Make sure that you have a system in place to *gain feedback from satisfied and dissatisfied customers*. This system will provide crucial information that will help you to provide great customer service.

What do you do when the product or service *initially* falls short of the customers expectations? You have to make it right as soon as possible. *Resolving customer dissatisfaction* is one of the best ways to earn *long-term customer loyalty*.

What do you do when your product or service meets the customer's expectations? *Rewarding satisfied customers* is equally as important as being responsive to dissatisfied customers. Whether the rewards are in the form of referral bonuses, repeat customer discounts or just a sincere thank you letter, making customers feel appreciated is the key to creating loyal customers

Making a Customer Feel Welcomed, Appreciated and Valued can turn them into more than just a repeat customer. Satisfied customers become "Brand Ambassadors ". This type of devoted customers will advocate for your brand to their friends and family, which will magnify your company's marketing efforts.

This article is a companion to the **"Business Success" Video Series** presented by **Vince Rogers** for eHow.com

http://www.ehow.com/videos-on_12239455_business-success.html

VINCE ROGERS
Resources Management
& Communications Consultants
& ASSOCIATES   Learn about the **Keys to business Success** with help from the **Principal Change Agent** at **Vince Rogers & Associates** www.vincerogers.biz

Disguised Limits

Discover Life's Unlimited Opportunities!!!!

How to Run a Successful Outbound Telemarketing Sales Operation

by **Vince Rogers**

An *Outbound Telemarketing Sales Operation* is an organization in the business of marketing their products and services to prospective customers by making sales calls directly over the telephone. A Successful Outbound Telemarketing Sales Operation must combine:

- High-Quality Sales Prospecting

- Excellent Sales and Customer Service Training

- Conducive Call Center Sales Environment

A good sales call to a bad prospect is just a wasted opportunity. Reaching the correct prospects with your sales calls in a Successful Outbound Telemarketing Sales Operation will depend on Developing Quality Sales Leads. The Key to Generating Good Sales Leads is selecting them based on Good Target Marketing Research. You can do this by either Conducting Market Research Yourself or you will need to Buy Sales Leads from Another Company.

To the prospective customer Every Sales Call is made by the Company not by An Individual. Therefore it's important that you Hire Employees Who can be Trained to Represent Your Company Well over the telephone. Every effort must be made to provide your employees with:

- Detailed Product Knowledge Training

- Effective Sales Training

- Good Customer Service Training

Outbound Telemarketing Sales Operations take place in a "Call Center". The key elements of a good call center work environment that is conducive to effective selling are:

- Hiring Good Management and Training Personnel

- Providing Comfortable Work Stations

- Purchasing Adequate Telephone Equipment

Also, there are laws that cover the selling of certain products over the phone such as investments. You will need to familiarize yourself with these laws depending on the product that you are selling.

Above all, the keys to running a successful "tele-commerce" business will depend on:

- Whether you are Selling a product or service that is well suited to be sold over the telephone

- Whether you're attempting to sell to actual prospect s

and

- Whether you've hired and trained an effective telephone sales force

This article is a companion to the "Business Success" Video Series presented by **Vince Rogers** for eHow.com http://www.ehow.com/videos-on_12239455_business-success.html

VINCE ROGERS
Resources Management
& Communications Consultants

& ASSOCIATES

Learn about the **Keys to business Success** with help from the **Principal Change Agent** at **Vince Rogers & Associates** www.vincerogers.biz

Disguised Limits

Discover Life's Unlimited Opportunities!!!!

How to Make the Most of Newsletter Marketing

by Vince Rogers

A Marketing Newsletter can be a great way to stay in touch with existing and prospective customers. The Purposes of a Marketing Newsletter are to:

- Stay in touch with existing and potential customers

- Provide them with useful information about sales, product updates, special promotions and other useful information

- Exchange information that helps to reinforce the existing customer relationship

Some visitors to your retail store or website may not have an immediate need for your product or service. Getting potential customers to sign up to receive your newsletter allows you to continue building interest with prospective customers.

There are two things that happen every time someone signs up to receive your company's newsletter:

1) You get to collect information about prospective clients

2) You get to communicate the benefits of your product or service to them on a regular basis.

There are two keys to successful Newsletter Marketing:

1) Provide highly informative and engaging content

2) Include some kind of "Call to Action"

Your "Call to Action" is what Influences readers to either make a direct purchase or provide the company with additional information that influences later purchases.

Some examples of effective types of content are:

- Surveys

- Polls

- Contests

- Giveaways

- Video Tutorials

- Referral Programs

Newsletter Marketing is a good source for Referrals. Newsletters often get re-circulated in their entirety or individual articles get emailed to friends and reposted on blogs and social media sites. Once again, the key to making this happen is by having high quality interactive content that people are compelled to share with their friends and family.

This article is a companion to the **"Business Success" Video Series** presented by **Vince Rogers** for eHow.com **http://www.ehow.com/videos-on_12239455_business-success.html**

VINCE ROGERS
Resources Management
& Communications Consultants

& ASSOCIATES

Learn about the **Keys to business Success** with help from the **Principal Change Agent** at **Vince Rogers & Associates www.vincerogers.biz**

Disguised Limits

Discover Life's Unlimited Opportunities!!!!

The Advantages of Using Blogging as a Marketing Tool

by **Vince Rogers**

There are great advantages to using Blogging as a Marketing Tool. It is one of the most cost effective and high impact ways to generate and distribute high quality content that promotes your product or service. If your company is not already blogging, the process to get started is fairly simple. The first step is to choose the platform you will use to publish your blog. There are quite a few popular *Blog Publishing Services* that can be used to create a high quality marketing blog.

It is crucial that your blog be well designed and full of high quality content. In order to be a useful marketing tool, your content must be engaging, interactive and informative. However, the most well designed and highly useful blog is useless without followers.

The best way to gain a *Large Loyal Captive Audience* for your blog is by regularly generating relevant *High Quality Content* and gaining followers by *Distributing the Blog Widely* to your target audience

You should circulate the Blog to:

- Your Database of *Current or Prospective Customers*

- Your Network of Followers on the Most *Popular Social Media Platforms*

- The most popular *Blog Directories*

Blog Directories are services that list popular blogs, much like an on-line index or card catalog to assist people looking to follow new blogs.

To get the most marketing benefit from your Blog:

- Use the blog traffic analytics provided by your blog publishing service to determine the readership patterns of your existing followers

- Use this data to help fine tune your blog marketing campaign

Make sure that your company information is easy to find on the blog and can be easily shared with the public:

- Provide links to your website

- Make "widgets" or "gadgets" available

Widgets and Gadgets are apps that link your blog to other websites. Your blog readers will place them on their social media pages, personal websites and personal blogs.

It is also important that you make your blog interactive and be responsive to the comments posted on your blog. *The comments generated by your blog followers can provide extremely useful marketing data*. The marketing information captured from the positive and negative comments your blog generates, the growing list of blog followers and the demographic information from your blog analytics will enable you to take full advantage of using your blog as a valuable, effective, dynamic marketing tool.

This article is a companion to the **"Business Success" Video Series** presented by **Vince Rogers** for eHow.com **www.ehow.com/videos-on_12239455_business-success.html**

VINCE ROGERS
Resources Management
& Communications Consultants
& ASSOCIATES

Learn about the **Keys to business Success** with help from the **Principal Change Agent** at **Vince Rogers & Associates** www.vincerogers.biz

Disguised Limits

Discover Life's Unlimited Opportunities!!!!

How to Make a Business Portfolio for a Presentation

by **Vince Rogers**

In your pursuit of new clients, your business will have to make effective presentations. An effective business presentation will include all of the relevant information and documentation that will impress a decision maker. Your goal is to make the prospect believe that they are making the right choice to hire your company.

What to include in your presentation portfolio will depend on whether it is being delivered in person or delivered electronically. If you are making a presentation in person, you will want to prepare some type of visual aid such as a PowerPoint Slide show. This will allow the audience to follow along as you present the other items in the portfolio. Any audio or video documentation of your company's accomplishments can be included in this PowerPoint presentation as well.

You should always include your Brochure and Business Card so that the prospects can refer to them after the presentation has ended. Examples of previous client work are an essential part of an effective presentation portfolio. Depending on your type of business you may include such examples as:

- Product Prototypes
- Posters

- Flyers

- Photographs

Documentation of any media coverage helps to make a strong presentation. You should include any:

- Books

- Press Clippings

- Articles

Include any radio or television interview recordings in your PowerPoint presentation.

References from previous clients are important to include in your presentation portfolio. References can be in the form of:

- Video testimonials

- Letters of reference

- Testimonials from multiple clients

Some other items you may include will depend on the stage of the decision making process and nature of the presentation. You may need to make Financial Information and your Business Plan available to prospective clients as well. Effectively presenting all of these elements in your Business Portfolio will make for a powerful and successful presentation.

This article is a companion to the **"Business Success" Video Series** presented by **Vince Rogers** for eHow.com http://www.ehow.com/videos-on 12239455 business-success.html

VINCE ROGERS
Resources Management
& Communications Consultants

& ASSOCIATES

Learn about the **Keys to business Success** with help from the **Principal Change Agent** at **Vince Rogers & Associates** www.vincerogers.biz

Disguised Limits

Discover Life's Unlimited Opportunities!!!!

How to Design a Consulting Business Brochure

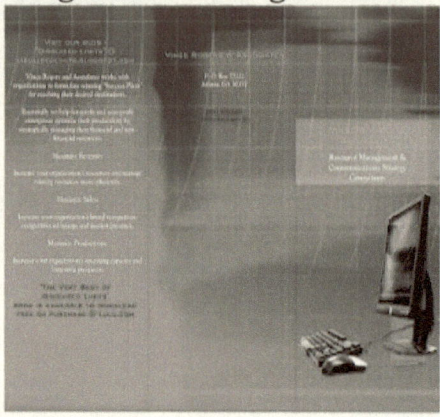

by Vince Rogers

Sometimes as a consultant it can be difficult to explain to a potential customer specifically what value you can bring to their business. Not even your excellent "elevator pitch", eye-catching business card or well crafted letter may be enough to seal the deal. A well designed Marketing Brochure for your Consulting Business can be the most effective tool that you have available to make an impression on a potential client and stand out from the competition.

An effective brochure for your consulting business must combine 4 vital elements to successfully communicate your marketing message:

• Attractive Images

• Clear Layout

• Simple Folding

• Strong Writing

Attractive Images will be the first thing that catches a prospects eye. It is what initially holds their attention. While images should be eye-catching, they must also be appropriate to the business that you are promoting.

The layout of your brochure must be clear. It must have a logical flow that enables it to be read easily. The reader must also be able to unfold and re-fold the brochure in a way that makes it easy to use over and over again.

The goal of a good brochure is to communicate a lot of important information without using a lot of words. Therefore, the writing must be strong, clear, logical and concise. Make sure that your vital contact information is prominently displayed and easy to read. Don't forget to include your:

• Mailing address

• Phone numbers

• Fax number

• E-Mail address

• Web Site address

Social Media Information

You want your brochure to stand out and be noticed. However, you should avoid using any fonts, graphics or colors that make the actual content difficult to read. You may decide to design the brochure for your consulting business yourself or you may use another company to produce it. In any event, you should pay careful attention to making sure that you incorporate all of these elements into making the most effective marketing brochure possible.

This article is a companion to the **"Business Success" Video Series** presented by **Vince Rogers** for eHow.com **http://www.ehow.com/videos-on_12239455_business-success.html**

VINCE ROGERS
Resources Management
& Communications Consultants
& ASSOCIATES

Learn about the **Keys to business Success** with help from the **Principal Change Agent** at Vince Rogers & Associates **www.vincerogers.biz**

Disguised Limits

Discover Life's Unlimited Opportunities!!!!

How Can Using Project Management Information Systems (PMIS) Give an Organization a Competitive Advantage?

by Vince Rogers

Your company just landed a much needed new project. Now you want to make sure that you do a great job for your new client. Your business needs to restructure the entire organization. Otherwise, your company will never move to that "next level". In order to give your organization a competitive advantage in the project management process, you may want to consider using a *Project Management Information System or (PMIS)*.

Project Management Information Systems help organizations to plan, execute, and close each phase of the project management process. They help assure that all of the appropriate steps are being taken at each project phase. They can be used to confirm that each project task is completed properly.

A Project Management Information System is defined as "An electronic information system that consists of the tools and techniques used to gather, integrate, and disseminate the outputs of project management processes. It is used to support all aspects of the project from initiating through closing, and can include both manual and automated systems". Organizations that don't use such systems can certainly be successful at completing projects.

Nevertheless, by using a PMIS you have a better chance of making sure that the Scope, Cost and Time goals of the project are met.

The fundamental purpose of a PMIS is to manage the flow of information between upper and lower management as well as the other stakeholders working on a project. Information is collected, synthesized and distributed via electronic and manual channels. The ultimate goal of streamlining the information sharing process is to minimize the allocation of time, money, and man-hours spent to complete a project.

For smaller projects or projects that involve routine processes that your organization has a lot of experience with, a PMIS may not be necessary. However for large projects, very important projects or projects where you don't have a lot of experience using a PMIS may be crucial. Making this determination requires the examination of other factors as well. Before purchasing a PMIS you must also take into consideration:

- Integration with your existing hardware and software

- Training for those people in your organization that will be using this new tool

- Whether making such an investment is cost effective for your organization

After taking all of these factors under consideration you may conclude that using a Project Management Information Systems (PMIS) will give your Organization the Competitive Advantage it needs to complete projects successfully.

This article is a companion to the **"Business Success" Video Series** presented by **Vince Rogers** for eHow.com **www.ehow.com/videos-on_12239455_business-success.html**

VINCE ROGERS
Resources Management
& Communications Consultants
& ASSOCIATES

Learn about the **Keys to business Success** with help from the **Principal Change Agent** at **Vince Rogers & Associates** **www.vincerogers.biz**

Disguised Limits

Discover Life's Unlimited Opportunities!!!!

How to Develop a Strong LinkedIn Relationship

by Vince Rogers

Developing strong relationships on *LinkedIn* can be very important to career and business success. LinkedIn has over 150 million registered users and is still growing. It is the most powerful professional networking site on the internet.

"Social Networking" sites allow users to mix business with pleasure. LinkedIn is a purely professional networking site. Therefore the ultimate goal of using LinkedIn is to develop strong relationships that help you to advance your professional objectives.

The first step to developing powerful relationships on LinkedIn is to *fully complete your profile page*. This will give your profile a better chance of standing out to potential connections. The key to any good relationship is that it be mutually beneficial. It should be clear to potential contacts when they look at your profile why they should want to build a professional relationship with you.

The Most Important Sections of your Profile to complete are the:

- Summary

- Experience

- Education

- Honors and Awards

Also, it is important that you emphasize results and skills, rather than dates and titles.

To start with you will want to add contacts that you know well and who know you such as:

- Former Employers

- Co-workers

- Professors

- Classmates

Each time that you add a new contact, you should write them a *recommendation* and then ask for one in return. Having recommendations will make your profile stand out to potential new connections more than anything else.

After you have acquired some contacts and recommendations, you should then join LinkedIn *Groups*. Make sure that you join groups in the specific areas of interest that you want to build your network. Now that you've joined the right groups, you share a common interest with some of the top people in your field. This will make it more likely that they will accept your unsolicited connection requests.

The best way to make a good connection is to be become a resource to them. Promote your contacts businesses. Put links to their sites on your websites and blogs. Write recommendations for them. Comments on their posts and answer their questions and polls.

Becoming a valuable resource to your LinkedIn connections creates a reason for them to want expand your relationship or to interact with you "offline". Escalating your relationship with influential connections beyond LinkedIn can be the key to landing your "dream client", promoting your business or landing a lucrative new project. By creating a powerful Profile, strategically joining the right Groups, acquiring the right Connections and Recommendations and becoming a resource rather than just a contact, you can build powerful LinkedIn relationships that can dramatically enhance your professional success.

This article is a companion to the **"Business Success" Video Series** presented by **Vince Rogers** for eHow.com http://www.ehow.com/videos-on_12239455_business-success.html

VINCE ROGERS
Resources Management
& Communications Consultants

& ASSOCIATES

Learn about the **Keys to business Success** with help from the **Principal Change Agent** at **Vince Rogers & Associates** www.vincerogers.biz

How to Develop a LinkedIn Relationship

eHow.com Featured Video

Watch @ http://www.ehow.com/video_12239462_develop-linkedin-relationship.html

and watch the full "Business Success" video series @

http://www.ehow.com/videos-on_12239455_business-success.html

Disguised Limits

Discover Life's Unlimited Opportunities!!!!

Reasons for the LinkedIn IPO

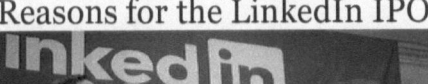

by Vince Rogers

LinkedIn is the most powerful professional networking site on the internet. The currently has more than 150 million registered users worldwide. The LinkedIn brand name has become as synonymous with professional networking as Google has become with searching the internet.

LinkedIn filed for an initial public offering in January 2011. They traded their first shares on May 19, 2011, under the NYSE symbol "LNKD". So why would a privately owned company that is experiencing astronomical growth and making tons of money for their owners want to "go public" and share the wealth with everybody else?

People start a business for many reasons. One of those reasons is that an entrepreneur has a great idea and they want to see their vision come alive and grow. At a certain point, the vision for the company grows to the point where expansion requires more money than the company can finance through loans, venture capital or profits.

When a company reaches that point they may decide to have an "IPO" or Initial Public Offering of shares of stock. "Going Public" as it is also commonly referred to, allows a greater number of large and small investors to invest in the company in return for a share of ownership. This enables the company to raise a lot of money for expanding the company without borrowing money that they might otherwise have to pay back.

Although this sharing of ownership interest decreases the original owner's stake in the company by a certain percentage, the increased financial investment in the company will multiply the value of the company many times over. So in general, a company is able to raise a lot of money to expand the company, while giving up some control of the business. Specifically, in the case of LinkedIn there were other advantages to "going public" that should create long term benefits for the company.

LinkedIn's ability to successfully complete an IPO in a bad economy showed a sign of strength that created an enormous media buzz. This positive attention resulted in the company gaining wider recognition and an increase in customers, revenue and profits. Also, LinkedIn's ability to have an IPO first allowed them to beat perceived competitors such as FaceBook, Twitter and direct competitors such as Viadeo to the punch. This positioned them as a leading brand amongst similar companies, a stronger company than their competitors and signaled a perceived vote of confidence from "Wall Street"

When your great idea becomes the next LinkedIn, these are the types of strategic and competitive factors that you should also consider before deciding to have your successful IPO.

This article is a companion to the "Business Success" Video Series presented by Vince Rogers for eHow.com http://www.ehow.com/videos-on_12239455_business-success.html

Learn about the Keys to business Success with help from the Principal Change Agent at Vince Rogers & Associates www.vincerogers.biz

The Big Fundamentals

Disguised Limits

Discover Life's Unlimited Opportunities!!!!

The Big Fundamentals

Success Planning

"In order to convert passion into positive achievement, it is necessary to have an organized strategy for transforming that passion into purposeful action"

~ Vincent L. Rogers

Success Planning Fundamentals

Good Research
leads to > > > >

Sound Planning
leads to >>>>

Effective Strategy
leads to >>>>

Communications
Fundamentals

Choose the right audience

Choose the right message

Choose the right channel

Choose the right time

Branding Fundamentals

Build **Identity**

Maintain **Consistency**

Focus **Outreach**

Marketing Fundamentals

Grab Attention

Build Interest

Stimulate Desire

Take Action

Project Management Fundamentals

Determine the Scope of the Project
– What exactly are we doing????

Determine the Costs of the Project
– What exactly will it cost????

Determine the Duration of the Project
– Precisely how long will it take????

Determine the Deliverables of the Project
– What exactly should we produce????

Evaluate the Risks of the Project
– What could possibly go wrong????

Evaluate the Rewards of the Project–
Precisely what value will be created????

www.vincerogers.biz

The Big Fundamentals Mobile App

Access to quick reminders for the "The Big Fundamentals" of Success Planning when you're on the go

Free download to your phone: In your Mobile browser go to
http://mobilemags.mobi/14722

(data charges may apply)

Within the **mobilemags.mobi** site you can use **'Quick download Code'** which is: **14722**

Vince Rogers & Associates, LLC

VINCE ROGERS

Resource Management &
Communications Strategy
Consultant

VINCE ROGERS &
ASSOCIATES
WWW.VINCEROGERS.BIZ

P. O. Box 77222
Atlanta, GA 30357
404-939-0261

vincerogers@vincerogers.biz
twitter.com/vincevision
disguisedlimits.blogspot.com

PLEASE CONTACT US TO FORMULATE A
WINNING
"SUCCESS PLAN"
FOR YOUR ORGANIZATION
VINCE ROGERS & ASSOCIATES
WWW.VINCEROGERS.BIZ

www.vincerogers.biz

Vince Rogers is an experienced resource manager and communications strategist. He is academically trained in economics, marketing, project management and professional communications. He is a graduate of the **Andrew Young School of Policy Studies** where he studied under such noted economists as **Dr. Donald Ratajczak**, the South's best-known economist. He possesses many years of successful experience in financial services and real estate management and marketing.

He is the **Principal Change Agent** at **Vince Rogers & Associates** www.vincerogers.biz

He has been profiled in such business media outlets as **Atlanta Business RadioX** on the shows **High Velocity Radio** http://highvelocityradio.businessradiox.com/?p=1061 and **Write Here, Write Now** http://writeherewritenow.businessradiox.com/?powerpress_pinw=198-podcast in the book **Publishing as a Marketing Strategy** (BookLogix Publishing Services, 2011 ISBN: 9781610051149) and in the prestigious upcoming **2013 Pfeiffer Annual: Consulting** (John Wiley, 2012 ISBN: 978-1-1182-7379-1)

He is the publisher of **Disguised Limits** @ http://disguisedlimits.blogspot.com which is **#2** on Networked Blogs.com **Top Blogs in the Opportunities category.**

He is the **Atlanta Personal Brand Examiner** @ Examiner.com and the Host of the eHow.com **"Business Success" Video Series** @ www.ehow.com/videos-on_12239455_business-success.html

"The Very Best of Disguised Limits"

Volume 1 is available to buy or download free @ http://www.lulu.com/product/16215088

Selected **LinkedIn** Recommendations for Vince Rogers

"Vince Rogers has been a trusted business partner and friend for the past 30 years. He is one of the most brilliant and prolific writers in the United States. He is known internationally as an intellectual, author, economist, poet, novelist, columnist, essayist and political pundit. He has published several highly acclaimed books and blogs on business leadership and success. Vince has worked with me as a government consultant, real estate investor, communications advisor and literary critic. Vince has also unselfishly worked with me in the non-profit sector and has been a source of great personal strength to me personally. I recommend Vince Rogers wholeheartedly for any venture that requires leadership, scholarship and ingenuity."
Roland Lane, Jr., President, Earth Harvest Real Estate, LLC

"Vince Rogers as host of Business Success on eHow.com took complex management ideas and turned them into succinct concepts for aspiring Warren Buffets to use as guides in their day to day operations. He was always prepared. Very easy to work with, committed to his profession. Vince is the embodiment of a management executive, who will take on any project and give it the focus that will assure a successful conclusion"
Edward Castner, Owner, Crewsix Productions

"Vince reported to me when I was the Sales Manager at Lehman Brothers in Atlanta up until 1993. Vince was always extremely reliable and I could count on him to get the job done with very little supervision. Additionally, Vince was always very prompt with any written reports and other information that I needed. His peers and the brokers in the office respected and liked him. He was the "go to guy" when things needed to get done. I highly recommend Vince."
Jeff Diamond, *Managing Director, JP Morgan*

"Vince Rogers is truly a light in a dark world. I had the pleasure of meeting him during a time of challenge in his life and watched how he not only searched within himself for inner strength, but offered the same to his family and friends. I have also found him to be very conscious and concerned about the happenings of the world. His global perspective is fresh and his keen insight is only matched by his generous heart. I consider Vince a mentor, a confidant and a friend and I strongly recommend him for any position he pursues.
Keith Somerville, *Pastor, St. Johns Downtown UMC*

www.linkedin.com/in/vincevision

Disguised Limits

Discover Life's Unlimited Opportunities!!!!

Resolve

success

doesn't always depend on coming up with **the *very best idea,***

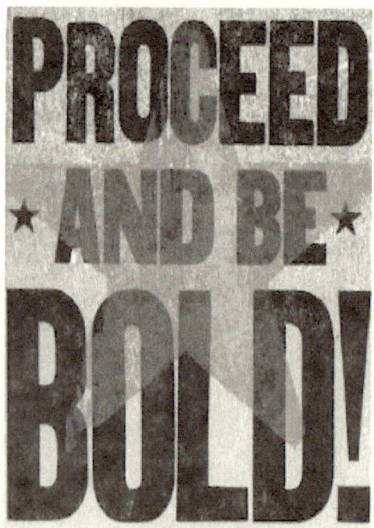

Sometimes it's just a matter of **putting *your very best* into the** *idea that* **you** *come up with.*

~ Vincent L. Rogers

Take Note

www.ingramcontent.com/pod-product-compliance
Lightning Source LLC
Chambersburg PA
CBHW021902170526
45157CB00005B/1926